RIGHTFUL TERMINATION: AVOIDING LITIGATION

Richard Stiller
Ron Visconti

A FIFTY-MINUTE™ SERIES BOOK

CRISP PUBLICATIONS, INC.
Menlo Park, California

RIGHTFUL TERMINATION: AVOIDING LITIGATION

Richard Stiller
Ron Visconti

3 3113 01351 6606

CREDITS:
Editor: **Sara Schneider**
Typesetting: **ExecuStaff**
Cover Design: **Carol Harris**
Artwork: **Ralph Mapson**

Copyright © 1994 Crisp Publications, Inc.
Printed in the United States of America by Bawden Printing Company.

English language Crisp books are distributed worldwide. Our major international distributors include:

CANADA: Reid Publishing, Ltd., Box 69559—109 Thomas St., Oakville, Ontario Canada L6J 7R4. TEL: (416) 842-4428, FAX: (416) 842-9327

AUSTRALIA: Career Builders, P.O. Box 1051, Springwood, Brisbane, Queensland, Australia 4127. TEL: 841-1061, FAX: 841-1580

NEW ZEALAND: Career Builders, P.O. Box 571, Manurewa, Auckland, New Zealand. TEL: 266-5276, FAX: 266-4152

JAPAN: Phoenix Associates Co., Mizuho Bldg. 2-12-2, Kami Osaki, Shinagawa-Ku, Tokyo 141, Japan. TEL: 3-443-7231, FAX: 3-443-7640

Selected Crisp titles are also available in other languages. Contact International Rights Manager Suzanne Kelly at (415) 323-6100 for more information.

Library of Congress Catalog Card Number 93-73119
Stiller, Richard and Ron Visconti
Rightful Termination: Avoiding Litigation
ISBN 1-56052-248-8

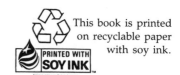

This book is printed on recyclable paper with soy ink.

ABOUT THIS BOOK

Rightful Termination: Avoiding Litigation is not like most books. It has a unique "self-paced" format that encourages a reader to become personally involved. Designed to be "read with a pencil," there are exercises, activities, assessments and cases that invite participation.

This book is designed to inform managers about how to avoid litigation when faced with the necessity of terminating an employee, and informs the reader how not to hire the type of person who might sue the company if terminated. It deals with how to avoid terminations, if possible, by effectively dealing with problems with employees as they arise. Finally, *Rightful Termination: Avoiding Litigation* takes managers through the process of a legally correct, or "rightful," termination, to protect the organization from possible litigation.

Rightful Termination: Avoiding Litigation (and the other self-improvement books listed in the back of this book) can be used effectively in a number of ways. Here are some possibilities:

- **Individual Study.** Because the book is self-instructional, all that is needed is a quiet place, some time, and a pencil. Completing the activities and exercises will provide valuable feedback, as well as practical ideas for improving your business.

- **Workshops and Seminars.** This book is ideal for use during, or as pre-assigned reading prior to, a workshop or seminar. With the basics in hand, the quality of participation will improve. More time can be spent practicing concept extensions and applications during the program.

- **College Programs.** Thanks to the format, brevity and low cost, this book is ideal for short courses and extension programs.

There are other possibilities that depend on the objectives of the user. One thing is certain; even after it has been read, this book will serve as excellent reference material that can be easily reviewed.

ABOUT THE AUTHORS

Ron Visconti, with an M.A. in Adult Education, has over 19 years' experience in career development, marketing, education and human services. Voted Career Counselor of the Year by the California Career Guidance Association in 1990, he is the founder and executive director of the Community Career Education Center, a private nonprofit career development center. He serves on numerous boards and advisory boards, including the Private Industry Council and the Regional Occupational Program. He is also a part-time instructor for the College of Notre Dame as well as community colleges and adult schools. Mr. Visconti is the co-author of *Effective Recruiting Strategies* (Crisp Publications).

Richard Stiller has over twenty years' experience as a Human Resources Professional and a manager of people. He is intimately familiar with both the hiring and the termination process. Over the past 15 years he has worked for such well-known Bay Area companies as Atari, Pacific Telesis, Electronic Arts and Borland. Currently he is a Human Resources Manager for Sun Microsystems Labs. In 1988, collaborating with Ron Visconti, Mr. Stiller co-authored the audio tape *Winning the Interview: Getting the Job You Want.*

PREFACE

For the manager of a company, whether large or small, the possibility of having to terminate an employee exists at all times. With that possibility comes the risk that the terminated employee will decide that he or she was unfairly treated and that the company should be sued.

The 1990's workplace is highly litigious, and sooner or later most managers will face the prospect of a law suit. *Rightful Termination: Avoiding Litigation* was written to help today's managers cope with our increasingly legalistic society.

Legal issues are often intimidating and complex. This book is designed, not for lawyers, but for the everyday manager. The case studies are based on actual cases and are designed to highlight issues that are fairly common in the workplace. Questions and authors' responses are included to involve the reader and to help him or her apply the principles to his or her situation.

Rightful Termination: Avoiding Litigation has a philosophy of common sense and takes a pragmatic approach. It makes good business sense to avoid legal confrontation; treat your employees fairly and you will probably avoid litigation.

We hope that this book will be useful in avoiding problems *before* they occur, as it is much easier and more cost-effective to deal with problems internally than it is to solve them in court.

Richard Stiller

Ron Visconti

Dedication

We wish to thank Eve Young for her invaluable support and expertise in making this project happen. We also thank Attorney-at-Law Bill Quackenbush for his astute legal counsel and for his insightful contributions to this book.

CONTENTS

INTRODUCTION

Today's manager is faced with a myriad of issues, from motivating workers to creating effective teams. Perhaps the most complex and sensitive of all a manager's tasks is what to do about employees who are not performing. Poor and/or difficult employees are *industry-free*. In other words, they are found in all industries (retail, manufacturing, government, insurance). Wherever there are human beings, there will be difficult employees.

In some instances, a poorly performing employee can be salvaged. Marty Brounstein addresses this equally complex issue in his book *Handling the Difficult Employee*. Issues in his book include how to turn around poor performance and set the employee on the right track, and how the beginnings of poor performance might be avoided at the start if the manager conducts an effective personnel selection search.

Most managers, however, are reluctant to face the unavoidable—the termination of a nonsalvageable employee who might have been working for the company for many years. It is the philosophy of the authors of this book to try all possible means to retain good employees. But there will be instances when no matter how many steps have been taken, termination is inevitable.

This book addresses what you, as a manager, can do to effectively fire such an employee before his or her poor performance affects the entire organization.

Please note: this book is not a substitute for legal advice. If properly used, however, it should help you save thousands of dollars in legal advice fees, by helping you prevent or deal with problems before they become legal issues.

We live in a very litigious society that resolves its conflicts in court. Although the legal world does shape our judgments in hiring and firing, we do believe that managers should not be intimidated by making important decisions that affect the company's future.

It is the job of the manager to consistently and fairly deal with employee issues. *It is the absence of fairness and consistent treatment to all that creates problems that can lead to unwanted legal consequences.*

INTRODUCTION (continued)

This book aims to empower the manager. After reading this book, managers should have a better grasp of how and when to terminate employees. The benefits of effective and rightful termination go beyond dollar costs. The good will and just reputation of a company can be maintained by fair practices, even when those practices include the necessary termination of poorly performing employees.

Termination is a management tool that, if used properly, can positively affect the profitability of the company.

The bottom line is, **how you minimize the risk of being sued.**

PART

I

Understanding
Rightful Termination

QUIZ: ARE YOU AT LEGAL RISK?

Analyze whether or not your management style puts you at legal risk for wrongful termination. Please answer "yes" or "no" to describe how you currently perform as a manager. Your honest answers will help you determine the amount of risk you face of being sued.

After taking the quiz, read on to find out what your score means and its legal implications.

_____ 1. Do you have each employee sign a waiver of application stating that he or she may be terminated at any time for any reason?

_____ 2. Do you have performance reviews with your employees on a regular basis?

_____ 3. Do you implement your own termination policies consistently for all those affected?

_____ 4. Do you hold several discipline meetings with difficult employees before you terminate them?

_____ 5. Do you document all of your disciplinary actions?

_____ 6. Do you use a progressive disciplinary plan?

_____ 7. Do you consult with a human resources professional or legal counsel before you terminate an employee?

_____ 8. Are you familiar with state and federal laws affecting termination?

_____ 9. Do you avoid using words such as "permanent employee" or "long-term employee" when offering a job to a new employee?

_____ 10. Do you get nervous at the prospect of firing an employee?

_____ **Total Score**

Give yourself three points for each "yes" answer. Add up your points and write your score at the end of the quiz.

The one exception is number 10. Number 10 has no legal consequences for you as a manager or for your company. The fact is that most managers do not want to fire an employee. In fact, a certain amount of nervousness might be appropriate when you are considering all the necessary steps to take to terminate someone.

WHAT YOUR SCORE MEANS

Twenty-seven is a perfect score. You have a good grasp of the concepts of termination. You now must consider whether you honestly take all of these steps. If you do, you are the model manager. You strive to treat all employees fairly and equally at termination, and you are not likely to face legal accusations that would stand up in court. If an employee sued you for wrongful termination, he or she would probably have no case.

A score of 21–27 indicates some degree of legal risk. A ''no'' answer to any one of the questions could put your company at risk for a law suit. You might review the issues covered in each question to which you answered ''no,'' and read the appropriate chapters carefully.

A score of 20 or below demonstrates a very problematic approach to termination. You need to examine your company's policies, practices and understanding of employment laws, and read this book carefully. Share it, as well, with others in your company.

TERMINATION MYTHS AND REALITIES

Every managerial issue has its own particular set of myths and realities. This section will describe some of the common myths of termination and dispel those myths by describing the realities.

MYTH: Managers rarely feel guilty about firing an employee.

REALITY: Most managers are very uncomfortable with firing, and even with discipline. It is human nature to want to avoid dealing with problems. This is, in fact, called avoidance behavior. Sometimes the ''nice guys'' give the message of desired change too late, when it is difficult to modify employee performance.

MYTH: Firing an employee does not benefit the employee; instead it will undoubtedly hurt his or her career.

REALITY: Firing is a common practice. Just because a worker has been fired doesn't mean his or her career is over. In an era of high turnover and intricate legal restrictions on the information an employer can reveal, it is hard to determine the reason an employee has left a job. These days most employers state only employment dates and the title of position in reference checks. Therefore, being fired is not as devastating as it once was for an employee.

MYTH: A manager can fire anyone, any time, for any reason.

REALITY: Yes and no. In *''at will states,''* managers can terminate anyone, any time, for any reason. This does not apply, however, to *unlawful termination*, which will be discussed in detail later. All companies must comply with state and federal regulations and avoid treatment that negatively impacts racial/ethnic, religious, age and sex groups. The business reasons for which an employee may be terminated anytime include performance, attitude and downsizing.

TERMINATION MYTHS AND REALITIES (continued)

MYTH: Terminating an employee does not impact the workforce.

REALITY: How you treat your terminated workers has a strong effect on the workforce. If a worker has been treated fairly and respectfully, the survivors will view their company positively. Lack of notice and unfair treatment, on the other hand, intensifies problems; the workers internalize conflicts, and morale drops throughout the company.

MYTH: Employees are usually happy to see a poorly performing employee leave.

REALITY: Many managers may have liked the employee even if he or she did not perform well. To some extent, they may have accepted the poor performance if it did not affect them directly. The main issue, however, is how the termination was handled. Workers will remember this. They tend to forget the bad performance of the worker and remember the likable person.

MYTH: Keeping one employee who performs poorly will not affect the entire workforce very much.

REALITY: Keeping a bad employee has a negative effect on existing employees. It sends a clear message to your present workforce, resulting in:

- Poor morale

- Frustration among good performers

- A message rewarding bad performance

MYTH: Terminated employees are always angry at their former employer.

REALITY: Terminated employees, like all of us, run the gamut of emotions. Elisabeth Kubler Ross, in *On Death and Dying*, discussed the emotional stages of dying. Job loss elicits similar stages. Not all workers are angry. However, most workers are experiencing loss, a sense of helplessness, and in some instances, depression. The laid-off worker should be treated with respect and dignity, and listened to with empathy.

MYTH: Terminated employees will not actually take legal action.

REALITY: Although only a small percentage of laid-off workers actually resort to litigation, the process is time-consuming and costly. It only takes one case to bog your company down in litigation fees and lengthy proceedings. Preventative medicine is vital; doing your homework can combat possible legal battles.

MYTH: Minorities and special groups should be treated differently and separately when they are terminated.

REALITY: Companies should treat minorities and special groups fairly, just as they treat all their employees. If a business decision is made and applied fairly, and documented that it was in fact a fair decision, a company cannot be intimidated by possibilities and immobilized by fear. Decisions, however, must be based on performance and reflect the goal of worker productivity and business performance.

MYTH: Once a person has passed a probationary period, he or she cannot be fired.

REALITY: Passing probation is no guarantee of permanent employment. This is why it is important, in both your policy manual and job offers, to avoid using language that implies permanent employment. An employee can be terminated anytime for performance or business reasons. The caveat is documentation!

MYTH: It is easier to terminate an hourly employee than a salaried employee.

REALITY: The circumstances surrounding firing an hourly employee might appear to be more basic. However, rules of common sense should apply to handling the termination of any category of employee.

8

TERMINATION MYTHS AND REALITIES (continued)

MYTH: Legal counsel is necessary for all terminations.

REALITY: A lawyer is not needed in all termination cases. Of course, caution and a review of procedures is always advisable. We recommend a conservative approach. If the situation gets sticky or complex, legal advice is a safe bet. It is important to safeguard your company's interests.

MYTH: If an employee is not performing adequately, it is wise to get rid of that person immediately.

REALITY: Most of your employees are salvageable. Think of the time and money you have invested in each employee. An organized and systematic approach to evaluating performance can ''rehabilitate'' many employees. Think of the positive rewards of saving a poorly performing worker, and think of the time and money you will save by not having to replace that person and train a new employee.

MYTH: Seniority affects the likelihood that an employee will be terminated.

REALITY: Seniority should not be the basis of employability; performance should be. This advice is for companies not bound by union agreements.

MYTH: It is best to terminate an employee at the beginning of the day.

REALITY: There are several advantages to terminating a worker at the end of the day. You avoid the ''uproar syndrome'' which has a domino effect. Terminating an employee at the beginning of the day tends to disturb other workers, which might be unproductive. Termination at the end of the day allows the worker to leave quietly and with dignity.

ABOUT TERMINATION:
AN INTERVIEW

The following interview with Attorney-at-Law Bill Quackenbush was conducted by Ron Visconti.

QUESTION:

What rights do terminated employees have?

ANSWER:

The primary categories that employers need to be concerned about are:

PUBLIC POLICY
DISCRIMINATION
CONTRACTS

Public policy concerns situations where employees are terminated because they have either exercised legal rights such as jury duty or right-to-tell-the-truth in some government investigation, or they have tried to obey a law or assert a legal right. Perhaps an employer asked an employee to do something that is arguably not lawful. If the employee believes it to be unlawful, refuses to engage in that kind of conduct, and is terminated for that, the employee may have a claim against the employer for wrongful termination. The employee does not necessarily have to prove that the conduct would have been illegal. It may be enough that the employee simply show that he thought it was unlawful and had a reasonable basis for thinking that. This area poses a financial risk to employers, because if an employee can establish a termination based upon violation of public policy, then the employee can recover not only any lost income but also damages for emotional distress.

Discrimination is probably one of the more important areas nowadays for several reasons. First, if the employee can establish discrimination in connection with the termination, recoverable damages would include, again, not only lost income and emotional distress damages, but also attorney's fees. The employee does not have to prove that his or her age, sex or race was the *sole* reason for the termination, only that age, sex or race played what the courts call "a determining factor" rather than "the major factor" in the termination. Second, more of the work force is over age 40, which is a protected category. One of the first questions we ask people is, "How old are you?" If they've hit age 40, it is possible that the employee was discriminated against in part because of age.

AN INTERVIEW (continued)

It is actually fairly common for the employee to be the subject of discrimination, but yet not realize it. For example, a 50-year-old may be terminated and told his position is no longer necessary, and then a month or two later he is replaced in that same position by somebody who is age 25. That is evidence of discrimination. The employee does not necessarily know what is going on at the time of termination, so very often we will wait to assess the situation.

Contracts is the third category. In theory, this would be a lesser concern to employers, because the damages an employee can recover in a contract case are generally limited only to lost income. However, it is a lot easier to establish a contract claim than any other kind. Contract claims generally fall into three categories.

First, an employee can establish that some written promise of the employer has been violated. For example, a promise set forth in an offer letter, which has led to the employee's acceptance of the job, was not fulfilled.

The **second** catagory is implied contracts, which generally involve employees who have been at a job for at least a few years and, because of promotions, commendations, company practices and policies or combinations of these things, believe that they would be terminated only with ''good cause.'' It is not required that the employer actually had promised that it would terminate only with ''good cause.'' Instead, it is a question of whether under all of the circumstances the employee had reason to believe that termination would be only for ''good cause.''

In this case, the employer must establish that it did have good cause to terminate the employee. It is not enough under the law for the employer simply to operate in good faith. For instance, if an employer terminates an employee for misconduct, the company may have to prove that in fact this did happen. Moreover, the employer should always tell the truth when terminating an employee. An employer may think, ''No one can prove what I really said in that meeting, so I'll just deny it.'' Maybe no one can establish exactly what was said in the meeting, but it is easy to show that the employer's credibility is suspect and therefore its version of what went on in that meeting is not to be believed.

The **third** kind of contract in wrongful termination cases is called a covenant of good faith and fair dealing. What this means is that even an employee who does not have an implied contract is entitled to be treated fairly and honestly. In practice, this means that company employment policies—and practices that may not be in writing, but are the accepted ways that the company does business—must be applied uniformly to all employees. If the company doesn't follow that policy or practice with respect to one employee, the employee may have a case for violation of good faith and fair dealing. For example, if a company usually provides a spoken or written warning for a minor matter, such as being late for work, but then terminates one employee for the same infraction without the warning, that may very well give rise to a violation of good faith and fair dealing.

QUESTION:

What are some of the attributes of an interesting case?

ANSWER:

Interesting cases are winnable cases, which most likely will be discrimination cases, cases involving long-term employees, and cases where the employer has lied to the employee. Certainly a major factor in any case is the employee's loss or potential loss of income as a result of termination, which particularly applies to workers in their 40s, 50s or even 60s. But the factor of recoverable damages of lost income or emotional stress makes a case more appealing, because we must be able to recover the cost of litigation if the case gets that far. In a discrimination case, the law permits you to recover attorney's fees in any reasonable amount regardless of the size of the damages recovered by the employees, because attorneys are encouraged to take these cases just for the ultimate goal of eradicating discrimination in society. Thus, discrimination cases in particular can be very expensive for an employer to lose, because they pay the employee's damages, the employee's lawyer and their own lawyer.

AN INTERVIEW (continued)

QUESTION:

Many companies are laying off workers. What advice do you have for employees terminated in this situation?

ANSWER:

First, the employee's attorney must determine if the layoff really was a reduction in force. Sometimes an employer will claim that an employee has been terminated because the position was eliminated, but in fact the company did not really reduce its workforce. Typically, one or two positions are eliminated at the same time the company is hiring. A court will not view that as a legitimate reduction of the work force.

Moreover, even in a genuine layoff, the employer does not have free rein under law to pick out individuals arbitrarily that it believes should be terminated. The selection process has to be fair and nondiscriminatory. For example, if a manager selects 10 people for layoff, of which two of these are the two oldest workers in the department, that manager and that company may have a legal problem. The employer should provide managers with fair and nondiscriminatory guidelines for layoffs, and a committee should review the selections on a companywide basis to make sure that there has been no discriminatory impact.

QUESTION:

Is it enough that an employer undertake an action in good faith?

ANSWER:

Not necessarily. If the employer engages in what amounts to discrimination—if it picks primarily older employees for termination, for example—that may be unlawful. Case law supports the notion that even unconscious discrimination can be illegal, so employees do not have to prove that the employer was consciously picking out the older employees. If, in fact, that's what happened, the employer might be in trouble under the law.

Employees may have other rights in layoffs. For example, employers may be obligated to transfer their laid off employees to available positions in the company. If they don't, particularly if many older employees are terminated, the company may be charged with discrimination. One common tactic we have seen, though, is that employers will shuffle their favorite people—often the younger ones—into safe positions before they do their layoffs. Then they will say honestly to the terminated employees that no other positions are available. The problem with that picture, of course, is that the employer has made sure no other positions are available, because they have already been filled with younger employees. That's not going to work under the law.

QUESTION:

When can an employer be liable for wrongful termination, even though there hasn't been any termination?

ANSWER:

Sometimes employees say that their employers are making life difficult for them. Companies don't want employees to sue if they are terminated, so the employer harasses them, hoping the employees will quit. Employers often think that means employees won't have any case against them. They're wrong.

Under the law of constructive discharge, any time an employee is forced to quit, such that any reasonable person in that position would have quit, the law will treat that employer as having actually terminated the employee. The employer cannot avoid liability by saying, "The employee quit."

Suppose an employee was told, "Your performance is poor. We're putting you on probation and creating certain standards that you must meet. If you don't think you can meet the standards, maybe it would make sense for you to quit." It happens the standards were impossible to meet, so the employee did quit. Now the company is arguing that it did not terminate this employee, so it has no liability. However, the employer may have liability because it created the situation where the employee was forced to quit. If the employer can prove that the performance really was poor, then the employee cannot win solely by proving that he or she was forced to quit. One of these other independent legal theories must still be proved to show wrongful termination. Constructive discharge simply covers the situation in which the employee has not truly been terminated by the express statement of the employer.

AN INTERVIEW (continued)

QUESTION:

To what extent can employers protect themselves?

ANSWER:

Employers can use an employee handbook, and if they do, they will be forced, under the law anyway, to honor the commitments in that handbook. Many employers believe that if the handbook says that employees can be terminated at any time for any reason then companies are off the hook for any kind of termination problems. That idea is false. The law continues to hold those kinds of clauses invalid, if other evidence indicates that the employer has made commitments to the employee. For example, if the handbook says, "I can fire you at any time for any reason" on page one, and on page 10 it says, "Our general practice before termination is to give first a written warning, then a final warning and then termination," that is a contradiction. "At will" language will not be given any weight in that situation.

P A R T

II

Hiring Impacts Firing

FINE-TUNING THE HIRING PROCESS

The easiest way to avoid firing a poorly performing or difficult employee is during the selection process. In other words—*don't hire him or her in the first place!*

A key point to remember: *As a manager, you'll never have more control over a potential employee than during the hiring process.* It's far easier to eliminate a potential problem up front than to try to deal with problems that occur later on, after the hire has been made.

Step 1: Develop a Preinterview Strategy

► Have Candidates Fill Out a Job Application

Always have candidates fill out an application before the interview begins. An effective application will have a waiver declaring that the candidate recognizes that if hired, he or she can be terminated "at will." Termination "at will" means that the employee can be terminated for any reason at any time, as long as the reason does not discriminate against age, religion, or sex. *The candidate should always sign and date the application.*

If your company is not currently using an application, it is important that you adopt the use of an effective one immediately. Boiler plate applications are available from most business supply or stationery stores. You might also find one that is used by a well-established business in your geographic area, provided it can "pass muster" legally.

Generally, companies that have done a lot of hiring will have an application form that has been refined and reviewed by legal counsel. You might want to obtain sample application forms, design one to suit your particular needs, and then have it evaluated by your attorney.

The candidate's signed waiver on the application is one of the most effective preventive measures any business can take to avoid legal action for wrongful termination.

FINE-TUNING THE HIRING PROCESS (continued)

► Carefully Review the Job Application

Once the application has been completed and signed, the hiring manager should take time to review it carefully. *If the candidate does have a resume, review it also and compare it to the application.* Always have the candidate fill out the job history portion of the application even if he or she has a separate resume.

► Prepare Your Interview Questions Ahead of Time

It is important to decide exactly what information you need to decide that a candidate is qualified. The best way to ensure that you get this information is to know what questions you are going to ask before the interview.

List your questions on paper and bring them with you to the interview. Make sure not only that you ask the candidate all the questions you have listed, but also that he or she answers all the questions you ask. It is important for the hiring manager to control the interview. Knowing ahead of time what questions will be covered and what answers are necessary ensures that control.

► Allow Enough Time for the Interview

Set aside enough time and an appropriate place for the interview. How much is appropriate for an interview? The longer you spend with a candidate, the better chance you will have of finding out his or her qualifications. Some managers claim they don't have much time to interview. Many sandwich interviews between other appointments. They often start the interview late and still must finish it on time to get to their next appointment, thus short-changing the applicant and denying themselves the chance to learn as much as possible about the candidate.

When a manager spends enough time interviewing a candidate, he or she saves time later. A manager may spend two hours interviewing an applicant. This may seem excessive, but managers rarely have the luxury of spending only two hours dealing with a poorly performing employee. In fact, between verbal and written warnings and weekly meetings to review performance, a manager may spend as much as 20–30 hours dealing with this issue. A two-hour interview may well save you much more time later on.

A manager should spend no less than one full, uninterrupted hour interviewing, regardless of the level of the position. If the interview is going well, the time should be extended to two hours. Whenever possible, the hiring manager should keep his or her schedule open after the interview so the interview can be extended, if necessary, to better learn about the candidate and his or her qualifications.

Interviews should be held behind closed doors, in offices or conference rooms. Phone calls should be handled so as not to interrupt the interview. *Interruptions break the flow of questions and keep the hiring manager from getting necessary information.*

Step 2: Evaluate the Resume

The application and the resume should contain much of the same information; consistency is one thing you should look for. Here are some guidelines for evaluating a resume, and some questions that you should ask about each.

▶ Resume Checklist

Before an interview, review the candidate's resume for the following "alarm" signals:

- What concerns or questions does this resume present?
- Are there any unexplained gaps in the dates?
- Has the applicant changed jobs frequently?
- What are the reasons for his or her job changes?
- Are there any unusual changes in job function or title?

SAMPLE RESUME AHEAD

FINE-TUNING THE HIRING PROCESS
(continued)

Sample Resume

Daniel Tyler
101 First Street
Los Angeles, CA 90101
(213) 555-2144

Career Objective: MARKETING

1992–1993   **Megalectronics; Ojai, CA**
Sales Representative
Sold $350,000 of electronic equipment
Part of a team of sales reps. whose accounts totaled over
$2 million in business
Knowledgeable in electronic computers

1990–1991   **Corcoran Co.; Bakersfield, CA**
Sales Manager/Telemarketer
Trained, motivated, and managed six sales mgrs.
Developed over 25 new leads per month
Trained sales reps. in technical aspects of product sales

1989–1990   **ZAR Inc.; Pasadena, CA**
Sales Manager
Managed a sales force of 10 sales reps.
Accounted for $1 million of computer hardware sales
Increased sales volume by 20%
Voted Manager of the Year 1990

1985–1987   **Ultra Machines; Westwood, CA**
Sales/Office Manager
Worked with major corporate clients
Oversaw the workflow of 14 sales reps.
Responsible for the accounts payable/receivable functions

Education

1981–1983:   Los Angeles City College; Los Angeles, CA

Resume Reading Exercise

List your four major concerns raised by this sample resume:

1. _____

_____

2. _____

_____

3. _____

_____

4. _____

_____

Answers:

1. There are unexplained gaps in employment. (All time should be accounted for, including education and time between jobs.)

2. The dates do not include months.

3. There is evidence of frequent job changes—job hopping.

4. The candidate's job function changes from manager to sales representative (downward mobility).

Review:

The information on the resume and application will probably suggest some of the questions the hiring manager should ask during the interview.

FINE-TUNING THE HIRING PROCESS (continued)

► **What You Are Looking For**

Gaps in employment: Gaps in employment might indicate that the candidate was either fired or laid off from his or her last job.

Inconsistencies between the resume and the application: Some candidates put false information on resumes to enhance their work history and experience. Often such candidates forget to make sure that the resume and the application match.

Reasons why a candidate left previous jobs: A good application includes a question next to each job history that asks why a candidate left his or her former positions.

Step 3: Be Cautious During the Interview

► **Find Out Why Candidates Left Previous Jobs**

Spend time learning why the applicant left former jobs. Always ask the candidate to go into detail about why he or she left a company. What did he or she think? What triggered the decision to move? Was he or she told to look for another position? Answers to these questions will tell the hiring manager a lot about a candidate's performance and motivation. Be wary of answers like:

- *"It was a mutual agreement."*
- *"My boss was threatened by my abilities."*
- *"The job they hired me for changed."*
- *"It was political."*

Ask the candidate to be specific. Why was a mutual agreement necessary? What specific events took place that led to the mutual agreement? Who initiated the agreement? What political change caused him or her to leave the job?

Don't accept the answers to these questions at face value. Make the candidate qualify his or her responses. Make sure that you have a very clear idea of the *real reason* why he or she left the company.

While it is illegal for a manager to ask candidates about any prior legal problems they have had with former employers, such issues may surface in a thorough interview process. If an applicant has had legal conflicts with several companies he or she has worked for in the past, the hiring manager might want to avoid hiring him or her.

Some candidates, of course, have had bona fide legal complaints, but many others look for problems hoping they will make money from settlements with companies who prefer not to go to court, even if the company is not at fault, to avoid bad press.

Exercise

List five appropriate, probing interview questions, phrased to elicit as much information as possible about a candidate's past job experiences and his or her expertise in your company's field.

1. _____

   _____

2. _____

   _____

3. _____

   _____

4. _____

   _____

5. _____

   _____

FINE-TUNING THE HIRING PROCESS (continued)

► **Do Not Make Statements That Could Be Interpreted As Offers of Job Permanence or Security**

Positions are never really permanent. Use phrases like "full-time" or "regular." Comments that seem to promise long-term employment can be used against an employer in court. Even comments that allude to a promise that a candidate will be assured of a job as long as his or her performance meets qualifications can be construed as a contract for continued employment.

► **Think Ahead**

Always be thinking about what would happen if you hire this candidate and then found out that he or she was not qualified to do the job. Terminating an employee is an unpleasant process for both the manager and the person being fired. Often the employee, the same person who put his or her best foot forward during the interview, will be very angry if terminated later on and angry employees often seek legal counsel, especially if they are being fired. They will remember anything said that might be construed as a promise.

Stick to talking about the position, the company and the applicant's qualifications.

► **Avoid Discriminatory Comments or Questions**

Often candidates will overlook comments about race, religion or sex during an interview. But later, if they are being terminated, they will recall these same statements and use them against you in court. Statements or questions about the following increase your legal exposure and should be avoided:

- Marital status
- Sex/sexual orientation
- Transportation (unless the candidate's own transportation is needed as part of the job)
- Age/height/weight/medical condition
- Family status/childbearing/pregnancy
- Country of origin of applicant or parents (unless U.S. citizenship is a qualification of the job)
- Religion/religious holidays observed

> IT IS IMPERATIVE TO STICK TO QUESTIONS AND COMMENTS
> THAT EXPLORE *ONLY* THE CANDIDATE'S ABILITY TO DO THE JOB.

► Have Candidates Interview with Their Potential Co-workers

The most effective way to do this is to set up a schedule of 30–60 minute interviews. The benefit of this is that the hiring manager will get other people's input on the viability of a candidate. Each interviewer should be prepared to cover specific pre-planned questions so that the hiring manager can have a more thorough idea of the candidate's qualifications.

Step 4: Follow Up After the Interview

► Get Co-Workers' Feedback After the Interviews

Hold a post-interview meeting with everyone who has been involved in the process. Allow everyone to express an opinion. Don't shortchange this part of the process since wise hiring ensures good employer/employee relationships.

► Conduct Reference Checks

This is an important step that many hiring managers skip because they think that references will only give good information because they are handpicked by the candidate, or that company policy will not allow the references to give them any significant information at all.

Skilled interviewers, however, will not hire a person without first checking his or her references. They also know how to obtain valid references.

First, always ask the candidate for references who will talk to the hiring manager. The burden for this must rest on the candidate.

Second, never be afraid to do "backdoor" references. Backdoor references are people you know or someone in your company who has worked with the candidate in the past who can give you an honest appraisal of his or her qualifications.

A reference is only as good as the questions you ask.

FINE-TUNING THE HIRING PROCESS (continued)

These are good reference questions:

"Tell me about the candidate's strong points."

"How did this person work with others? Give me some examples."

"Where did you feel that the candidate needed to improve or grow?"

"Would you work with the candidate again?"

"How well did the employee get along with his or her manager? Give some examples."

"Why did the candidate leave the company (or would want to leave the company)?"

"If fate intervened and you had to *work for* this candidate, what would be your concerns, if any?"

"To the best of your knowledge, what were this person's greatest accomplishments on the job?"

"What were the biggest disappointments about the candidate's performance?"

"What kind of manager did this person work for?"

If the reference *was* the manager, ask him or her to describe his or her managerial style.

► Hold a Second-Round Interview

If, after following these steps, you still have doubts about the candidate call him or her back for another round of interviews. Express your concerns about his or her ability to do the job. And if, after all of this, you still are not convinced, pass over the candidate and move on to another applicant.

Some job candidates are simply inclined to be litigious. In other words, they are prone to look for problems, to document "evidence" against an employer, and ultimately, to attempt to bring a lawsuit if they feel they have been mistreated.

Ten-Point Early Warning Alert

Watch for these possible "warning signs" of such a candidate:

1. The candidate cannot give you a satisfactory reason for leaving a former company, or the reason he or she gives does not coincide with the reason his or her references give.

2. The references the candidate has given will not talk to you.

3. The resume and application do not match, and the candidate cannot adequately explain the variance between the two documents.

4. The candidate has a history of legal problems with former companies.

5. The candidate spends a lot of time during the interview expressing concerns about the company's fair treatment of employees.

6. The candidate has a long background as a union activist. (While it is the legal right of an employee to belong to a union and participate in union activities, an overly active role in such activities may mean that the candidate is inclined to resort to lawsuits to solve problems.)

7. The candidate refuses to fill out and sign the application.

8. The employee insists on seeing a written job description early in the interview process.

9. The candidate is contentious or aggressive during the interview.

10. The candidate makes comments that could be construed as discriminatory.

WHEN IN DOUBT, DO NOT HIRE!

FINE-TUNING THE HIRING PROCESS (continued)

Step 5: Making the Offer

When the hiring manager has decided to make an offer to a qualified candidate, he or she can help avoid potential legal conflicts by following these guidelines. (See the sample offer letter located in the appendices at the end of the book.)

► **Use an Offer Letter**

Always express the terms of the offer in the form of an offer letter signed by the hiring manager. Make sure that your offer letter template has been reviewed by legal counsel. (An example of a good offer letter has been included in the appendix.)

► **Use "At Will" Statement in Offer**

Always make sure that the letter includes an "at will" statement about the candidate's employment with the company.

► **Avoid Expressing Salary as Annual**

Always express the candidate's salary in hourly, biweekly, or monthly terms. Expressing a salary in annual terms can imply a contractual obligation on the part of a company to pay a terminated employee a year's salary at the time of separation.

► **Use an Introductory Period with New Employees**

Consider adding an introductory period to any extended offer. An introductory period allows the company to terminate an employee for any legal reason without going through a performance improvement plan. A typical introductory period is 60–90 days.

► **Use Language Involving Employment Time-Frames Cautiously**

When extending the offer verbally, avoid statements that could be construed as a promise of long-term or lifetime employment. Never tell the prospective employee that he or she has a job for life or that you look forward to many years of working together. Even seemingly innocuous statements like these can come back to haunt an employer legally.

► **Have Employee Sign Offer Letter**

Insist that an employee sign the offer letter before he or she begins his or her employment.

Case Study: THE CANDIDATE

Part One

John Campbell was running late. He knew that he had a candidate waiting in the lobby to interview for the marketing position that had opened up when a long-term employee had left the company. In fact, one of the reasons John was so busy was that he now had to cover two jobs as a result of this employee leaving.

John had originally allowed over an hour for the 11 a.m. interview. He figured that if the candidate looked good he could extend the interview and take him to lunch. However, a crisis took until 11:30 to resolve. Now, 30 minutes late, John realized he had only 30 minutes to talk to the candidate.

"Sorry about the delay," John said quickly, as he extended his hand.

On the way to his office John spoke about how busy things were because he was down an employee. Dan nodded but said little.

The top of John's desk was covered with papers and files. He sifted through the papers looking for Dan's resume. Having given no thought to the questions he was going to ask, he figured that he would "wing it" through the interview, but with less than thirty minutes he doubted he would be able to get the information he needed to make a decision.

"I brought an extra copy of my resume," Dan offered.

"My schedule is not normally like this," John said, scanning the resume.

John noticed that Dan had jumped around among jobs quite a bit and there was no evidence of a college degree.

Before he asked his first question the phone rang. John had forgotten to forward calls to his secretary. He told Dan that he would just be a minute. Five minutes later he hung up the phone. Now he had 25 minutes in which to conduct the interview.

"So tell me about yourself, Dan." John probed.

FINE-TUNING THE HIRING PROCESS (continued)

Dan rattled off his recent work history, which approximated what was on his resume.

John pretended to listen but actually he was thinking about his next meeting. Every now and then he nodded and smiled at Dan.

Finally he forced himself to concentrate on Dan. "What are you doing for lunch?" he asked.

"I have no plans," Dan answered.

"Good," John said. "I'm going to ask several of my employees to take you to lunch. After that we'll see where things go." "Is that OK with you, Dan?"

John went to the office next to his and returned with Gina.

"This is Gina Tobey, Dan. She works in product marketing. She and Jim Gable are going to take you to lunch."

Taking Gina aside, John said, "Give me feedback on Dan. He seems to be very qualified. If you and Jim like him I might make him an offer."

Gina nodded. "Should I see you right after lunch?" she asked.

John shook his head, asking, "How about later in the day?"

The lunch went fine. Unfortunately, neither Gina or Jim had a resume and Dan had given his last copy to John. Dan spent most of the lunch asking questions about the company and its products, which gave both employees plenty of time to talk about themselves and their views and accomplishments.

By the time lunch was over, Gina and Jim felt pretty good about Dan. It was as if Dan had been hired, and was one of the team.

Later in the day Gina sat in John's office extolling Dan's virtues. "I think we should hire this guy before someone else snaps him up," she said. "He's passed muster with our department. Let's put together an offer."

Dan accepted the offer. John and his department were ecstatic. Personnel was surprised when John showed up the next morning and told them that he had made an offer. They expected to be in on the hiring process, especially concerning salary approval and ensuring that references were checked. Now they had no choice. The offer had been made, so they had to stand behind the commitment John had made to Dan.

"John," the personnel director asked, "Did we do references on this guy?"

"Didn't have time," John shot back at her. "We had to move on this guy. I was afraid I'd lose him. Besides, the team was sold on him."

"Did you find out why he left his last job?" she continued. "On his application he said it was to look for better career opportunities. It seems strange," she continued, "for him to leave his old job voluntarily without another position lined up."

The personnel director expressed her concerns to the vice president of finance and dropped the matter. She hoped that Dan would work out. She had no vested interest in seeing him fail.

Exercise

1. List specific mistakes John made in this interview._____

_____

2. To avoid this type of hiring situation in the future, list a few hiring policies this company should insist on._____

_____

3. If you were John, what steps would you have taken to ensure that you had enough time with Dan?_____

_____

4. Finish this story. What kind of experience will John's department likely have with Dan?_____

_____

(This case study will be continued on page 57.)

FINE-TUNING THE HIRING PROCESS (continued)

Authors' Response:

A number of mistakes were made in this interview, including:

- *Not allotting enough time for the interview*

- *Not being prepared for the interview*

- *Not giving full attention to the interview (allowing interruptions, being preoccupied with other matters, not listening closely to the candidate)*

- *Relying on the inadequate input of others*

- *Not conducting a reference check*

- *Not scheduling more interviews*

- *Being too hasty in making a decision*

While this scenario is very typical, it is a prime example of how less-than-careful hiring practices may lead to legal problems later on. Let's hope that Dan really was a good employee and that John made the right decision. However, warning signals, such as inadequate answers about why he left his old job, and his lack of a college education (which was desirable for the position), lead one to think that Dan may not have been the best candidate for the job. But considering the poor hiring process, Dan might have grounds for legal action if he is terminated later.

Remember: An ounce of prevention . . . !

P A R T

III

Taking Disciplinary Action

DISCIPLINARY ACTION

To avoid having to terminate employees, it is certainly best to avoid hiring difficult workers in the first place. But when a difficult employee does emerge, how you handle the situation can make the difference between terminating and "rehabilitating" an individual, creating a productive worker.

Whenever an applicant is hired, there is a chance that it will be necessary to terminate this employee. There is no foolproof way to ensure that any person you hire will become a difficult employee. There are ways to minimize the risk of hiring such a person, but the bottom line is that whenever a candidate is hired, he or she is a potential difficult employee.

The first step is to ask what constitutes a problem or difficult employee. The difficult employee comes in many forms and works at all levels of the company.

Most importantly, a part of a difficult employee's work performance is unsatisfactory. The unsatisfactory work might be intermittent or frequent. If such work habits are tolerated, the manager has not only openly permitted bad performance to persist, but has also inadvertently reinforced such work habits and therefore greatly reduced the likelihood of changing the employee's performance.

It is important when observing and analyzing your employees' performance to be able to describe unsatisfactory behaviors or outcomes. Personality traits and attitudes not related to a particular behavior are hard to describe and therefore harder to document.

It is helpful to examine our own actions and our own part in creating the problem. Often we avoid a difficult employee situation developing under our management.

ARE YOU A PART OF THE PROBLEM?

DISCIPLINARY ACTION (continued)

Why We Ignore the Difficult Employee

► Sometimes the difficult employee is actually created by the manager. The employee was recruited and selected by the manager. It can be a sign of poor judgment that the manager has brought this problem (the employee) into the organization.

► The worker makes a great impression. The employee has a wonderful image in front of all coworkers as well as the manager. This worker can do no wrong.

► The manager hopes it will get better. Maybe if he or she doesn't handle this problem, it will get better or go away.

► The manager may ignore large parts of an employee's work. Managers will often accept skill deficiencies in their employees rather than try to correct or fortify weak areas.

► The manager may be uncomfortable with his or her role. Some managers have trouble disciplining employees. They feel they will no longer be seen as friends.

► No one wants to fire an employee deliberately. Some managers will go to great lengths to avoid this process.

► The difficult employee may show promise. Poor performance is sporadic, and so the manager may ignore it, hoping that the potential strengths of the employee will miraculously appear and offset his or her deficiencies.

► There may be times when the undesired behavior is minimal or appears to have gone away entirely.

Why Employees Don't Perform Up to Standard

Although playing psychologist is not your function, it is often helpful to understand why a problem is occurring. In his book *Handling the Difficult Employee*, Marty Brounstein lists 10 reasons that employees do not perform up to standard:

1. They do not know how or what they should do.

2. The reward or consequence is for not doing what they should do.

3. They think they are doing just fine.

4. They think their way, not your way, is better, but it is not.

5. There is no negative consequence to them for poor performance.

6. They have obstacles limiting their performance.

7. They do not want to do the job, or know why they should do it.

8. They fear a negative consequence.

9. They are, in essence, punished for doing what they are supposed to do.

10. They think something else is more important.

Exercise

Can you think of any other reasons, from your own experience, why employees perform poorly?_____

_____

_____

These reasons, along with the others that you have listed, may provide avenues for improving an employee's performance.

AREAS OF CONCERN

There are many traits or behaviors common to difficult employees:

► Not meeting any standards of the job that have been described to them

► Poor attitude

The following actions reflect a poor attitude:

- Dealing with the public or colleagues flippantly

- Being rude to customers

- Being uncooperative with coworkers

- Failing to follow instructions or guidelines

- Complaining frequently

- Carrying out assignments reluctantly

► Sloppiness and frequent mistakes

Although the employee has adequate training and instruction in his or her job, the same mistakes occur over and over again.

► Failing to complete tasks on time

► Not doing his or her fair share when the work flow is heavy

► Failing to meet goals or quotas important to your organization

► Tardiness and absenteeism

This behavior has a direct effect on the work of others. Being a punctual, reliable worker 90% of the time is not enough. Your consistent presence is needed.

► Drug abuse and alcoholism

Substance abuse cannot help but affect the work of the employee, and perhaps that of the other employees as well. It simply cannot be tolerated in the workplace.

► Inappropriate behavior

► Dishonest or unethical conduct

Exercise

1. Recall an employee from your past management experience who you found difficult to handle. Describe the employee's specific inappropriate behavior.

_____

_____

_____

_____

2. If you feel you waited too long to deal with the problem, why did you ignore this employee's behavior?_____

_____

_____

_____

3. After reading Marty Brounstein's 10 reasons why employees perform poorly, explain why the worker you just described probably failed to meet your company's standards._____

_____

_____

_____

THE DISCIPLINARY MEETING

When these examples of poor performance occur, the next step is to hold a disciplinary meeting.

The disciplinary meeting serves the following functions:

- To protect you, the manager, from a wrongful termination suit

- To increase communication between the manager and the employee

- To help define the problem and possible solutions

- To establish a clear time frame in which to solve the problem for all parties concerned

Before the Disciplinary Meeting

Before you have a disciplinary meeting, it is good to prepare for it.

Some Tips:

▶ Don't allow problems to expand. If you can nip the problem or undesired behavior in the bud, so much the better!

▶ Arrange a quiet time with no interruptions where both parties can discuss the problem. Try to conduct the meeting late in the day. If you hold the meeting too early in the day, the worker may stew over the problem throughout the day and exacerbate the situation.

Consider these openers:

"Joe, I want to talk with you about your work progress. Can you come to my office at 2:00?"

"Jill, I am worried about your having been twenty minutes late every day for the last two weeks. Can we talk about this on Wednesday at 4:00?"

Once you have started the meeting, you will need to practice THE ART OF LISTENING.

One of your key roles as a manager is to listen to your employees. You will need to listen very closely to learn why the employee is not performing well.

However, it is not important that you come to a conclusion about the cause of the employee's behavior. You are not a psychologist. The important thing is that a meeting has taken place, and that the employee has received the message that you are unhappy with his or her work and you want it changed in a specific way.

Active Listening Includes Three Main Components:

1. To be able to learn the emotional state of your employee in this situation:

> *"It sounds like you're angry."*

> *"It appears that you're unhappy with . . ."*

2. To be able to paraphrase what the employee is saying:

> *"It's been hard to get to work because you can't get your car started in the morning."*

> *"The child care center you use opens at 8:00 and you have trouble getting to work by 8:15."*

> *"It sounds to me that the buses don't come at convenient hours for you."*

3. To be able to summarize what has been said:

> *"You realize that you have been late and you now know that you need to take an earlier bus to get here on time."*

> *"So, you think by having Joe give you an extra day, the proofreading mistakes will be drastically reduced?"*

THE DISCIPLINARY MEETING (continued)

In active listening it is important not to blame. Using the word "you" tends to inflame the conversation.

Here's an example of what NOT to say:

"You always come in late for work."

A better way of putting it might be this:

"It worries me that you come in late for work. We're a small office and we rely on each other."

State your concern and then listen.

Review:

- Start off with a statement of concern.
- End with a specific performance improvement plan.
- Avoid blame and phrases like "you always" or "you never."

Exercise

Imagine a disciplinary meeting with one of your current difficult employees.

1. What specific work-related behavior would you like to see this employee change?_____

_____

2. When and where would it be best to hold this meeting?_____

_____

3. What statement could you make to open the meeting neutrally?_____

_____

4. Anticipate the employee's explanations and summarize a solution to conclude the meeting._____

_____

_____

WARNING SIGNS

There are numerous reasons why employees do not perform up to capacity and warning signs of problems. Most employees want to do a good job. So, why and how do employees get off track? The critical issue, actually, is not why, but how to improve their work performance.

Marty Brounstein, in *Handling the Difficult Employee,* lists common warning signs that a difficult employee may be "in the making":

1. **Output decreases.** The employee doesn't get as much work done. Sales or production is below normal.

2. **Work quality deteriorates. Errors increase.** His or her work is sloppy and sometimes incomplete.

3. **Employee misses due dates.** Assignments or projects are late or not completed.

4. **Employee shows little or no initiative.** He or she does not begin to work without being pushed or reminded.

5. **Employee avoids tougher tasks and assignments.** He or she puts off or complains about the difficult jobs. Often, the employee's effort goes into getting someone else to do the work.

6. **Complaints increase.** The employee considers decisions that are made, tasks that are worked on, and others' efforts to be wrong much of the time.

7. **Interaction with others decreases.** The employee turns quiet at meetings or more often works alone.

8. **Following and/or taking directions becomes difficult.**

9. **Defensiveness or irritability increases.** Having calm and rational conversations with the employee becomes more difficult. Mood swings become more pronounced.

10. **Cooperation diminishes.** Getting along and working with other employees becomes more difficult. Conflicts start to happen.

11. **Employee blames others for mistakes or failures.** He or she does not accept responsibility for his or her actions and is quick to find fault with others.

WARNING SIGNS (continued)

12. **Absences from his or her desk increase.** The employee is not around when he or she is needed, and often no one knows where to find him or her.

13. **Negative feedback from others increases.** Other employees or customers tell you about difficulties and disappointments they have had in dealing with your employee.

14. **Absenteeism and tardiness increase.** Knowing the precise reason for an employee's behavior is not as critical as how to improve his or her performance.

Performance Improvement Model

Here are five steps for improving worker productivity:

STEP 1   Identify and define the performance problem and how it has affected the work environment.

STEP 2   Find out why the problem exists.

STEP 3   Discover a solution to the problem.

STEP 4   Provide input, give guidance and offer criticism to the employee.

STEP 5   Write out a plan for improvement, with specific goals and objectives.

Let's use some illustrations of real live scenarios to illustrate what we're talking about.

Case Study: ERRATIC PERFORMANCE

Part One

Taylor is a 24-year-old junior accountant who has been working at his present company for 2 years. For the past 6 months, he has been coming in late and has been absent from work with increasing frequency. His manager for the past year is becoming increasingly concerned.

When Taylor *does* work, it is acceptable. However, lately he has indicated that he has some "personal stuff" going on.

After analyzing Taylor's work behavior, what would you, as his manager, do about the situation?

Authors' Response:

Put him on first verbal warning. Ask that he be present every day from 9 A.M.–5 P.M., and to not let his personal problems interfere with his work.

Part Two

Everything has settled down for a few weeks. Taylor is performing well. However, one day he comes very late, saying he has car problems. The next day he doesn't come in at all, at a time when an important project needs to be completed.

He says he had a bad day and he was too upset to come in. What and how would you intervene now?

Authors' Response:

Give him a 60-day written warning. Identify specific actions that he needs to correct. The written memo could go something like this:

Specific Actions That Need to Be Corrected

► You [the employee] must come in promptly every day, begin working at 9 A.M. and not leave before 5 P.M.

► If you [the employee] are sick for whatever reason, you must submit a doctor's verification.

► If you [the employee] cannot come in on time, you [the employee] must call ahead.

WARNING SIGNS (continued)

Part Three

After this written warning, Taylor's behavior is acceptable for about a week. Then, he doesn't come in and doesn't call. When he does finally come in, he makes an excuse about a traffic jam.

1. What must you do now as a manager?_____

   _____

2. What could the manager have learned through this episode? Or, are there any other possible management approaches to the problem of tardiness?

   _____

   _____

Authors' Responses:

Put him on final written warning. Stipulate he must not miss more than one day during the next six months or a year (specify). If he does, that will mean immediate termination from his job.

Perhaps the issue of tardiness could be handled by allowing an employee to work a shift later in the day.

A Bit of Basic Philosophy

► Most employees really want to do the right thing. Perhaps they are unaware of their unacceptable behavior and would be willing to change.

► Discussion between the manager and the employee helps to empower both parties. Hopefully, they will both come to a satisfactory agreement.

► The disciplinary process gives the employee an opportunity to improve.

► The process provides a tangible structure for positive change.

The Benefits of the Meeting

► It protects you, the manager (if you have done your homework).

► It defines a problem(s) that might not have been understood.

► It places the problem and its solutions in a specific, workable time frame.

► It provides consequences for actions or for goals not being met. For example:

"Failure to reach the above goals will result in . . . (be specific)."

Implement the Disciplinary Process

✔ DOCUMENT—DOCUMENT—DOCUMENT!

• Give concrete examples.

✔ Read your company's policy handbook and follow its practices.

✔ Take logical, sequential steps.

✔ Provide a reasonable time frame for improvement.

✔ Set up another meeting with your employee to review his or her progress.

✔ Have your documentation reviewed by a lawyer.

✔ Get examples of such documentation from other companies.

Case Study: A POOR ATTITUDE

Part One

Jim is a software engineer who works for a database company. Technically, he is very competent. This is his third job since he left college four years ago. For each job, his technical expertise has gotten him hired. He has been working at his present company for two years and is currently serving on his second team. But he doesn't get along very well with his other team members, and is often argumentative.

Jim's manager finds it hard to approach him about his attitude and work style. Instead, he asks Human Resources for advice. The HR manager tells Jim's manager that Jim is affecting the work of the team and must be told directly.

The manager arranges a meeting with Jim. He expresses his concern and talks about Jim's attitude. Jim blows a fuse. He leaves the meeting in a huff and doesn't come back. Jim stays home "sick" for the next two days.

Why did Jim blow up in the meeting and reject his manager's advice?_____

_____

If you were Jim's manager, what would you do at this point?_____

_____

Authors' Response

Give Jim a verbal warning. Even though he has had problems for the last two years, give him specific instructions. For example:

> *"Jim, you must work in your team without outbursts."*

> *"Jim, you need to listen to others without calling their ideas 'stupid' or 'impractical.'"*

> *"Jim, you must meet with Human Resources on a weekly basis to discuss your work progress."*

Part Two

Everything stabilizes until one day Jim misses his meeting with Human Resources. Jim apologizes, saying he was swamped and got consumed with his work.

About the same time, a new worker has been hired to assist Jim because he is falling behind in his work. Jim blows up.

If you were Jim's manager, how would you handle his behavior now?_____

_____

_____

Authors' Response:

Put him on a 60-day warning. Advise him of the consequences of his actions.

Part Three

Another week goes by and Jim blows up at his assistant. This time, Jim says he quits.

Are you at legal risk, as a manager?_____

Authors' Response:

No. You have taken all of the necessary steps and have documented Jim's progress.

Case Study: MARGINAL PERFORMANCE

Part One

Lea is a sales representative for a cellular phone company. She must sell 18 cellular phones per month. She reached her quota to pass probation, but ever since she was hired permanently, her sales have been slipping dramatically. Her work pattern includes taking off early and chatting excessively with her peers. She has weekly meetings with her sales manager during which she complains that she is not getting good leads and that it is a bad market.

The sales manager is getting pressure from the home office. She has repeatedly told Lea that she must meet her sales quotas and improve her work habits.

If you were Leas' manager, what would you do?_____

_____

Authors' Response:

Verbally outline several objectives for the next 30 days:

"Lea, you must meet your quota of 18 sales per month."

"Lea, you must sell 54 phones per quarter."

"Lea, you are expected to come in at 8 A.M. and are not to leave before 5 P.M."

"Lea, you must learn to manage your time more wisely." (Give some examples.)

Part Two

Lea starts to turn her performance around. Although she falls short of 18 phones, she has doubled her previous month's performance, from 8 to 16.

What would you do?_____

_____

Authors' Response:

Praise Lea and acknowledge her progress. Continue working with her to encourage continued success. Keep a progress sheet to record her performance.

SAMPLE PROGRESS SHEET

(Here is an example of a progress sheet that you might keep to document progress made between meetings with your employee to remind you of specific details to mention.)

DATE	REMARKS
June 1	Jill comes in at 9:30 A.M., one and one-half hours late.
June 15	Jill's projected budget draft contains five calculation errors.

Taking the necessary steps to successfully deal with the difficult employee requires the following:

► Great attention to detail (document, document, document)

► Effective and repeated communication with the employee (the disciplinary meetings)

► Extra attention to helping the employee improve his or her performance

This requires a considerable commitment from the manager, who will ultimately have to determine whether the employee is "worth saving." If the process is correctly followed, the manager will know that he or she has done a good job—everything possible to keep the employee and to ensure that he or she will perform well.

If the employee's performance still does not improve, the next step, of course, is the termination process, which you can begin with a clear conscience and with reasonable assurance that the employee does not have a legal case for wrongful termination.

P A R T

IV

Understanding the Grounds for Firing an Employee

CATEGORIES OF TERMINATION

There are three basic reasons why a company might rightfully terminate an employee:

1. PERFORMANCE
2. GROSS MISCONDUCT
3. ECONOMICS

We will examine each of these reasons in depth and give case studies to illustrate typical scenarios. We will also ask you to consider some questions related to each case study to help you avoid legal consequences from your actions.

It is important to understand the definition of each of the stated reasons, and how a company can be at risk legally if it is unable to justify a termination.

1. PERFORMANCE

For many years this was the most common reason for an employee to lose his or her job. It is the simplest concept. An employee is hired to do a specific job but cannot meet the minimum level of performance required to do the job to an acceptable standard.

There are different performance categories:

1. **The employee consistently does not meet the minimum standards expected for the job.**

   For example, a typist is expected to type 90 error-free words per minute, but consistently types only 60 words per minute and turns in work with numerous errors.

   An accountant who is expected to be proficient on electronic spread sheets in actuality has little working knowledge of them.

2. **The employee's personal work style does not fit that of the team or company.**

   Perhaps an employee is capable of getting the job done, but in the process alienates fellow employees by being pushy and aggressive.

   Another employee is disruptive and does not cooperate with fellow workers during projects and day-to-day tasks.

CATEGORIES OF TERMINATION (continued)

3. **The employee does not follow policies and procedures.**

   For example, an employee consistently circumvents a policy that requires certain levels of pre-approval. This might involve ordering office equipment or supplies, or even extending a job offer without an approved headcount.

4. **The employee is consistently tardy or misses work without valid medical reasons. He or she consistently comes to work late or takes days off without informing, or receiving the approval from, the manager ahead of time.**

5. **The employee is unable to meet specific, mutually agreeable objectives or goals.**

   A sales person might have a quota of $800,000 annually but is able to generate sales for only $450,000.

How can a company protect itself from legal action when terminating an employee for poor performance?

Reducing Legal Exposure

The following points are crucial to reduce legal exposure:

► Document in writing all job expectations, goals and objectives in a clear and concise manner.

► Have the employee sign and date the above documentation.

► Have written company policies and procedures.

► Have all policies and procedures reviewed by legal counsel.

► Apply all policies and procedures without regard to race, religion, age or sex.

► Use progressive discipline when dealing with employee performance-related issues.

In most states, employment policy is defined legally as "at will." This means that an employee can be terminated for any reason at any time as long as the reason is not based on race, religion, age or sex. Companies are wise to state their "at will" policy in the job application and the employee handbook. Employees must sign the application, plus a receipt indicating that they are responsible for knowing the contents of the handbook.

Regardless of any policy or "at will" statement, an employee can still attempt to sue a company for unlawful or wrongful termination. In matters concerning employee performance, companies are best protected by documenting the employee's performance problems, the fact that these problems were discussed between the employee and the manager, and the employee was given a reasonable time to correct the problems.

Case Study: THE CANDIDATE (continued from page 31)

Part Two

Dan Tyler's boss, John Campbell, was concerned. Dan had been an employee for three months, and yet he still seemed to need a great deal of day-to-day direction on simple department policies and procedures. Both of Dan's coworkers, Jim and Gina, had been in to talk to John about Dan's inability to carry his own weight. Both of them liked Dan personally, but felt that they were constantly covering for him or having to do his work to get a project completed.

Dan's resume had indicated that he was a very experienced professional, but when John asked Jim and Gina to rate Dan's experience level, they both responded that his level of performance, so far, was what they would expect of a new college graduate. In other words, Dan was unable to handle his present assignments and should be handling simpler tasks.

John's concern was that Dan was being paid for his apparent or expected experience. He was perplexed. Dan had seemed so good in the interview. He remembered, though, that the company personnel manager, Joanne, had been concerned because John had failed to do reference checks on Dan's past work performance.

CATEGORIES OF TERMINATION (continued)

Exercise

1. What should John's first step be?_____
_____

2. From whom should John seek advice?_____
_____

Authors' Response:

1. John should talk to the employee about his concerns regarding his performance. John should make these concerns very clear to Dan and actively listen to his response. John should not dominate this meeting. His goal should be to share the meeting time equally with Dan. This meeting is basically an information-gathering and communication session.

2. John should meet with the Human Resources manager and share the details of his concern about Dan's performance and the results of his meeting with Dan. John should make sure he understands procedures HR recommends in case the process calls for progressive discipline.

2. GROSS MISCONDUCT

Gross misconduct is the knowing and willful breaking of a company policy or procedure, or the knowing and willful breaking of a state or federal law while on the job. Gross misconduct can take place while an employee is either on the job site or conducting company business at any location.

Here are examples of gross misconduct:

- Stealing company products or equipment

- Using physical force against another employee

- Using abusive language

- Using or being under the influence of nonprescription drugs or alcohol

- Failing to report a criminal act by another employee within a reasonable time (varies per company, but usually three to five days)

- Possessing firearms or other dangerous weapons

- Gambling

- Falsifying or altering company documents, records or timecards

- Sexually harassing another employee

- Being dishonest

- Failing to adhere to safety rules and regulations

- Disclosing confidential company documents or information without authorization

Case Study: GROSS MISCONDUCT

Will seemed like an excellent employee. He was quiet, hardworking and always on time. If he was asked to work overtime, he always consented cheerfully. Working behind the cash register in a fast food operation could be a tough job, but Will never seemed to complain. He had been with the store for over a year and was a valued employee. His boss knew that he was having some financial problems, but Will never talked much about them at work.

Will's manager was bothered at times because the cash register came up short at least once a week. The money in the register did not match the money that was rung up in the day's sales. If the cash was short, though, it was usually no more than four or five dollars, and Will's manager let it pass.

One night the register was 25 dollars short. The manager checked the receipts and the cash several times, but each time it was the same. Finally she decided to assign each employee a register on each shift. Once they had finished their daily work, they turned in the receipts from their own particular registers and the manager checked the actual cash versus the receipts. The first day all the registers were fine, but on the second day Will's register came up 10 dollars short. Several days later Will's came up 20 dollars short.

CATEGORIES OF TERMINATION (continued)

Exercise

1. How can the manager prove that Will is responsible for the cash shortage?

_____

_____

_____

2. Once the manager has ascertained that Will is responsible, what should her next step be?_____

_____

_____

Authors' Response:

1. Assigning a register drawer to Will puts the burden of ensuring that the cash and receipts match on Will.

2. The manager should suspend Will on the spot and send him home pending an investigation. The manager could fire him on the spot, but she needs to have Will's final paycheck in hand before a termination can take place. The next step is for the manager to double check her evidence. If the evidence shows that Will is indeed responsible for the shortage, she should call Will back in (once Will's final paycheck has been cut) and terminate Will for gross misconduct.

Will should then be given a chance to return the money to avoid having the theft reported to the police. This should not be handled in a threatening manner. Let Will make the choice.

3. ECONOMICS

In the 1980s and 1990s layoffs have become a common occurrence in many industries. Even big companies like IBM and Apple Computer have finally had to resort to layoffs in order to reduce overhead as business competition has intensified.

Layoffs happen under different guises. Here are some examples:

► *Plant shutdowns*

This has become common in the automobile industry. Because of lagging sales, GM, Chrysler, Ford and others have reorganized and unified operations, shutting down regional production operations. Often key employees are offered jobs in another location. Other employees are given no other options and lose their jobs.

► *Financial needs of the business*

This is more common. The company generally is not going out of business or closing a plant. Its goal is simply to reduce overhead, because of poor revenues. The quickest way to do this is to trim the payroll. Often this is done through salary cuts or freezes. More likely, employees are laid off.

The following terminology is often identified with this act:

Reduction in Force (RIF) Employees are laid off with little hope of being rehired or picked up for another job within the company.

Rightsizing This is another version of RIF.

Available for Reassignment The employee's position is being eliminated or combined with someone else's position. In this case, the employee has a brief period in which to find another position within the company.

Redeployment This is another term which means Available for Reassignment.

Fired This has been the word used for many years when an employee has lost his or her job for any reason. Some veterans in the work force feel that all of the other language is simply a method of cushioning the stark reality of being fired.

CATEGORIES OF TERMINATION (continued)

Case Study: REDUCTION IN FORCE

Central Tool Works had just had their worst year in 30 years of business. They had a net loss of over a quarter of a million dollars, with twenty million dollars in total revenue. The senior management of the company met several days after the yearly financial reports had been published. After a long meeting they finally agreed to take an action that had never been resorted to during Central's 30-year history—a layoff.

Management decided to lay off 25 percent of the company's work force. This meant that 100 of their employees would be put out of work. Their biggest concern was that the layoffs be done fairly and equitably. Many of their employees had spent their working life at Central. Because management had always treated the employees fairly, any attempts from outside labor organizations to unionize Central had been met with little or no success.

Exercise

1. How should this company decide who to layoff?_____

_____

2. Who should be involved in the decision-making process of a layoff?_____

_____

3. How long should it take to make the decision about who will and who will not be laid off?_____

_____

4. What is the next step, after the layoff?_____

_____

Authors' Response:

1. The following criteria should be used to determine who will be laid off:

- *Ranking based on performance*

- *Length of time employed by the company*

- *Duplication of jobs*

- *A combination of all three*

2. All levels of management should be involved in a layoff decision. Each department should make recommendations to senior management. Senior management should be in close communication with all levels and departments throughout the process.

3. The layoff decisions should be made as quickly as possible. The rumor mill begins turning quickly, and productivity often suffers as a result. Therefore, it is best to minimize this consequence by acting quickly.

4. Meetings should take place (possibly company-wide, depending on the size of the company) to ''process'' the layoff with the rest of management and to set subsequent goals for the company.

If you have just one criteria, performance is the most critical.

PART

V

Avoiding
Legal Action

PROTECT YOURSELF

How can a company protect itself from legal action when terminating an employee for poor performance?

The following points are crucial to reducing legal exposure:

▶ Make sure that you *document all job expectations, goals and objectives in a clear and concise manner.* When we speak of documentation we are referring to *written documentation* preferably signed and agreed upon by the manager and the employee.

An annual or quarterly performance review is an excellent example of an opportunity to create this documentation. (See example located in the appendices at the end of this book.)

▶ Always *have the employee sign and date the above documentation.*

▶ Always make sure that *employees have a clear and concise plan that describes their goals over an expected period of time* (normally quarterly or annually). If their goals change then a new or amended document should be drawn up. *Once again, make sure that the manager and employee sign and date the document or plan.* (See example located in the appendices at the end of this book).

▶ Whenever possible, have written company policies and procedures. The policy handbook or manual should specifically cover the following topics.

Employee Handbook Guidelines

The following policies, clearly stated in an employee handbook, offer a great deal of protection to a company.

EEO Policy

This is a company's stated policy of Equal Employment Opportunity. It states that the company will not discriminate in its hiring practices based on age, sex or race.

PROTECT YOURSELF (continued)

Policy of Employment

This is a company's stated policy of the right to terminate an employee for any reason at any time, except for reasons of age, sex and race. This policy is often called "at will."

Hours of Work

This is not so much a policy about specific hours (such as 9 A.M. to 5 P.M.). This is a policy that states that an employee is expected to comply with all company working hour requirements, or be subject to disciplinary action.

Payment of Overtime

This policy states that the company complies with the FLSA (Fair Labor Standards Act), a federal law regulating hours of work, breaks and the payment of overtime.

Standards of Employee Conduct

This is a statement of expected employee conduct during work hours, which should be spelled out clearly in language that everyone can understand.

Unauthorized or Prohibited Employee Conduct

This is a description of conduct not acceptable during work hours, which includes abusive language, the use of physical force to harm another person, theft, falsifying information (such as a job application) and divulging confidential company information.

Termination

This, once again, is a restatement of the "at will" nature of employment and the company's right to terminate an employee, especially for reasons of gross misconduct, performance or economics.

Holidays

This is a policy specifically stating the federal and state holidays that are observed by the company.

Vacation

This policy explains the paid vacation employees can expect based on their length of employment with the company.

Sick Leave or Personal Time

This policy defines the amount of time that an employee can take off for sickness, medical treatment or personal business.

Leaves of Absence

There are generally two types of leaves:

► *Personal:* This is usually unpaid.

► *Medical:* This is usually covered by state disability, short-term disability and long-term disability.

PROTECT YOURSELF (continued)

Alcohol and Drug Policy

This policy defines the acceptable parameters of drug and alcohol use on company premises or during company work time.

► Have all policies and procedures reviewed by legal counsel to insure that they are legally within the guidelines of state and federal law.

► Apply all policies and procedures in an even-handed and fair manner regardless of position within the company, race, religion, age or sex.

► Follow a policy of progressive discipline when dealing with employee performance-related issues (see chapter 5).

► If the company needs to lay off employees, make sure that the criteria used to decide "who goes" is applied equally to all employees. Generally, the most successful criteria is based on a composite of performance and organizational needs of the business (duplication or elimination of jobs, etc.).

Employment in most states is "at will." This means that an employee can be terminated for any reason at any time, as long as it is not based on race, religion, age or sex. Companies are wise to state their "at will" policy in the job application and employee handbook. Employees must sign the application plus a receipt that they are responsible for knowing the contents of the handbook.

Regardless of any policy or statement of "at will," an employee still can attempt to sue a company for unlawful or wrongful termination. In matters concerning employee performance, companies are best protected by the following:

• document the employee's performance problems and the fact that these problems were discussed by the employee and the manager;

• and that the employee was given a reasonable time to correct the problems.

PROTECTED CLASSIFICATIONS

What is a protected classification?

Protected classes are individuals or groups of people who have, historically, been discriminated against by those who hold the majority of the middle or upper rung positions in the workplace.

The effect of this discrimination has been either to totally exclude members of these classes from entering the work force, or to prevent them from moving into higher paying, more responsible positions.

Government legislation has slowly forced a change in such practices. Legislation has mandated equality both in hiring and in termination practices. There are legal ramifications with any termination. But these legal ramifications are intensified when an employer lays off or fires an employee who belongs to what is known as a *protected classification*.

While federal law requires that all employees be treated equally in terms of opportunities and in the application of policy and procedure, there is still a representation gap between protected classes and the general work population.

Often companies try to close this gap through *affirmative action plans*. These plans represent an aggressive commitment to hire and promote minority and other protected individuals. Whether a company is truly committed to affirmative action or is trying to avoid legal consequences, such a plan can be effective.

The following are designated as protected classifications:

Women

As recently as one hundred years ago, women were excluded from most jobs. Men worked and women stayed home to take care of the family; there were few exceptions to this accepted way of life.

During the last half of the twentieth century, of course, much has changed. Women now compete equally (at least theoretically) with men in the job market. Men still dominate senior level positions in most companies, however (even though this is changing). This form of discrimination is called the ''glass ceiling,'' referring to the invisible career barrier that keeps women from the top jobs (and wages) in companies.

PROTECTED CLASSIFICATIONS (continued)

Physically Challenged

Workers with physical disabilities are now protected by the American Disabilities Act, which states that companies must provide equal access for disabled employees and nondisabled workers. Many companies are making a strong effort to hire physically handicapped (or physically challenged) people.

These are the major protected classes of workers that a manager must take caution to treat fairly. Individuals from these protected classes, and their lawyers, are particularly aware of discrimination issues right now.

Older Workers

While the purported rationale for age discrimination is the belief that employees beyond their physical peak can no longer perform tasks as well as younger and physically stronger employees, the underlying concerns are a perception that older workers are less flexible in their work habits, authority (a young manager might be intimidated by older workers), our ''youth culture,'' and the belief that younger workers will work for lower wages than older workers.

While age discrimination is an unfortunate reality in some companies, other companies actually find that older workers have better work ethics, are absent less and are generally more stable and valuable than many of their younger counterparts.

Physical stamina might have been a valid concern in the pre-industrialized society of 100 years ago, when many jobs were physically oriented. However, in the highly industrialized and automated environment in many companies today, this is no longer relevant.

The bottom line is that there is no rational reason for age discrimination. Perhaps there are even some real benefits to hiring workers with experience, stability and maturity—provided you don't discriminate against worthy younger candidates in the process!

Government legislation has made discrimination based on age illegal. And while age discrimination against any adult (over 18 years of age) is illegal, the widely accepted definition of this class is 40 years and older.

Ethnic Minorities

Ethnic minority groups feel that the best jobs go to Caucasians, and thus they are targets of discrimination. Government legislation requires companies to track interviews and hiring practices by both sex and race. While prospective employees are not required to report this information, most candidates and new workers do, in fact, fill out forms to track this data. While some progress has been made in legislating against discrimination, this is still a volatile area of employment and termination, and can be a very sensitive issue for a manager.

Credo of Rightful Termination

Here are some rules to think about and live by, similar in concept to the Golden Rule. They also make sense in avoiding legal consequences from terminating an employee.

1. Every worker is entitled to be treated with dignity and allowed to retain his or her self-worth.

2. All workers strive for fair treatment.

3. How you terminate employees will have an effect on those workers who remain with you.

4. Termination can be a process that strengthens a company and increases teamwork and productivity.

5. The ultimate goal of progressive discipline is to help an employee become a better worker.

6. The termination process is a learning experience for both employee and employer; it is a two-way process.

7. Termination can be just as important as hiring, and is just one of many management tools.

8. When you hire an employee, be aware that termination is always a possibility later on. Keep that in mind, in fact, in dealing with all employees.

9. To avoid legal consequences, remember that on-going communication is crucial, especially when a termination becomes necessary.

AFTERWORD

*The Golden Rule of Termination: Treat Your Employees
the Way You Would Like To Be Treated!*

There is much to be said for the "Golden Rule." It can be applied to most human interactions. As a manager, you are in the business of human interactions, as they relate to the running of your organization. An organization is, after all, a conglomeration, no matter how large or small, of people—human beings who have many basic similarities and a desire to be given a "fair shake" when it comes to their work performance.

As previously noted, *most* employees really do want to do a good job, and all they are asking in return is to be treated with respect and to be adequately compensated for their labor. Doesn't seem much to ask, does it? In the complex world of Corporate America, human interactions can get complicated, but really, it all boils down to treating your employees like worthwhile human beings who deserve decent treatment in the workplace.

- Hire smart.

- Train your employees well.

- Communicate.

- Investigate.

- Work with your difficult employees (try to bring them up to speed).

- And . . . if you do need to terminate them, do it fairly!

Termination is not a pleasant process, but litigation can become even more unpleasant than termination. It is time-consuming, messy, and VERY expensive. In short, it can be devastating for your organization. In these days of violence in the workplace, it can even prove fatal. Therefore, it is not only decent and correct to terminate your employees with just cause and to do it properly, it makes good business sense!

We hope that this book has been helpful in showing you the way to combine basic human values with smart business in order to avoid legal consequences, and that looking ahead to the possibility of termination will help you avoid it by dealing with problems before they become unmanageable.

—Eve Young

APPENDIX

Sample Forms

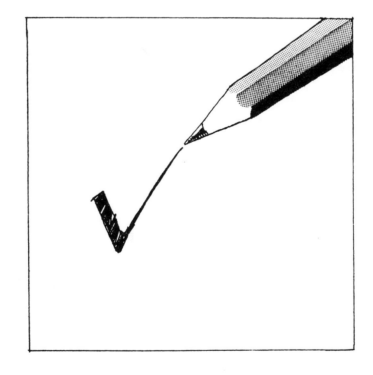

NONEXEMPT TELEPHONE REFERENCE CHECK

(from the legal point of view)

NAME OF CANDIDATE: _____

POSITION APPLIED FOR: _____

PERSON CONTACTED:_____ TITLE: _____

COMPANY: _____ CITY/STATE: _____

TELEPHONE NO. (H):_____ (W): _____

I'm calling to verify some information given to us by (applicant) _____, who is applying for a position in our company. How long have you known him/her?_____

What was his/her job title at your company?_____

What was the nature of his/her job?_____

What do you think of his/her work?_____

_____

How would you describe his/her performance in comparison with other people doing the same job?_____

How good were his/her written and oral communication skills?_____

Could you comment on his/her:

a. Attendance?_____

b. Dependability?_____

c. Ability to take on responsibility?_____

d. Potential for advancement?_____

e. Degree of supervision needed?_____

f. Overall attitude?_____

NONEXEMPT TELEPHONE REFERENCE CHECK (continued)

How well did he/she get along with management?_____

How well did he/she get along with peers?_____

What do you feel motivates him/her?_____

What are his/her strong points?_____

What are his/her limitations?_____

Why did he/she leave the company?_____

Would you rehire him/her? YES _____ NO _____ Why not?_____

_____

Is there anything you would like to add on your own?_____

_____

_____

_____

_____

_____

_____

_____

_____

_____

EXEMPT TELEPHONE REFERENCE CHECK

(from the legal point of view)

NAME OF CANDIDATE: _____

POSITION APPLIED FOR: _____

PERSON CONTACTED:_____ TITLE: _____

COMPANY: _____ CITY/STATE: _____

TELEPHONE NO. (H):_____ (W): _____

I'm calling to verify some information given to us by _____,
who is applying for a position in our company. How long have you known
him/her? _____

What was his/her job title at your company?_____

What was the nature of his/her job?_____

What do you think of his/her work?_____

_____

_____

How would you describe his/her performance in comparison with other
people doing the same job?_____

_____

How good were his/her written and oral communication skills?_____

_____

Is he/she a dependable person (i.e., meeting deadlines, getting to work on
time)? _____

How well did he/she get along with management?_____

How well did he/she get along with peers?_____

How well did he/she get along with subordinates?_____

EXEMPT TELEPHONE REFERENCE CHECK (continued)

What do you feel motivates him/her?_____

What are his/her strong points?_____

What are his/her limitations?_____

Why did he/she leave the company?_____

Would you rehire him/her? YES _____ NO _____

Why not? _____
_____

Is there anything you would like to add on your own?_____
_____
_____
_____
_____
_____
_____
_____
_____

SAMPLE OFFER LETTER

DATE

NAME
STREET
CITY, STATE, ZIP CODE

DEAR (Name):

We are pleased to offer you a full-time regular position with (Name of Company) as (Position Title). This position reports to (Name of Manager) within the (Department Name). Your first day of employment will be (date).

Your initial base salary will be ($0,000) per month, which equates to ($00,000) annually.

Your employment with (Company Name) will be for an indefinite term, and is ''at will.'' This means that you have the right to terminate your employment with us at any time. The company also reserves the right to terminate the employment relationship at any time.

This offer assumes that you have the legal right to work in the United States and can verify your eligibility for employment by producing acceptable forms of identification on your first day of work.

Please review this letter and, if it is appropriate, sign it and return it to us indicating that you accept the terms of this offer.

Sincerely,

(Signed Name of Company Representative)
(Printed Name of Company Representative and Title)

Accepted: _____ Date: _____

SAMPLE FIRST-STEP WARNING

Date: September 1, 19XX

To: John Smith

From: Bill Jones

Subject: Performance

The purpose of this form is to document the performance issues that we discussed during our weekly meetings on August 24 and August 31, 19XX.

The following are the performance issues that need correcting:

1. You have consistently arrived for work after the normal and expected starting time, which is 8 a.m. During the past two weeks, you have arrived on time for work only one day, which was August 25, 19XX. Your average late time for the other nine work days has been 15 minutes.

2. On August 24, 19XX, you did not return to work after the lunch break. You failed to call your supervisor and inform her of your reason for not returning.

3. On August 26, 19XX, you took an unauthorized break at 3 p.m., failing to get your manager's approval. Employees are normally allowed two ten-minute breaks during a shift, not including 30 minutes for lunch. All breaks over and above normal breaks must be approved by the manager in advance.

Expected changes in performance:

1. Be at your work station ready to work no later than 8 a.m. each workday.

2. Always inform and get approval from your manager in advance for any non-scheduled breaks or extended lunch periods.

Failure to take the above steps to improve your performance will result in future disciplinary action up to and including termination.

_____   _____
Employee   Date

_____   _____
Manager   Date

SAMPLE SECOND-STEP WARNING

Date: October 1, 19XX   From: Bill Jones

To: John Smith   Subject: Performance

The purpose of this form is to document the performance issues that we discussed during our weekly meeting on September 1, when you were given a first-step warning.

The following are the performance issues that still need correcting:

1. You have shown some improvement in arriving at work on time since September 1. On two occasions during the past month, however, you arrived late. On September 9 you arrived at work at 8:30 a.m., citing transportation problems. On September 23 you arrived at work at 8:15 a.m., this time citing traffic problems. In neither case did you call before 8:00 a.m. to inform your manager that you would be late to work.

2. On September 24 you did not come in to work at all. You finally called in at 11:00 a.m., stating that you were ill and had gone to see a doctor. Your manager asked you to document your visit by bringing a signed note from your doctor. You have, as of now, not produced the requested note.

Expected changes in performance:

1. You must be at your workstation, ready to work, by 8:00 a.m. each work day. If you are going to be late, you need to inform your manager before 8:00 a.m. You will also be expected to give your manager the time you expect to arrive.

2. You must produce a signed doctor's note for your absence on September 24 within three working days of this notice.

3. You have shown improvement in not taking unauthorized breaks as documented in the September 1 first-step warning. You must continue to take only authorized breaks and to receive approval in advance for all other breaks.

You will meet with the manager weekly to review your progress. Failure to meet any of these standards at any time during the warning period will result in immediate termination. This warning will cover a period of 60 days.

_____   _____
Employee   Date

_____   _____
Manager   Date

SAMPLE THIRD-STEP WARNING

Date: October 7, 19XX

To: John Smith

From: Bill Jones

Subject: Performance

The purpose of this form is to document the performance issues that we discussed during our weekly meetings on August 24, August 31, and again on September 1, 19XX, when you were given a first-step warning; and on October 1, 19XX, when you were given a second-step warning.

The following are the performance issues that still need correcting:

1. On October 6 you arrived at work at 8:10 a.m. You did not call in ahead of time as requested.

2. You did not meet the three-day deadline for producing a signed doctor's note documenting your absence on September 24.

Expected change in performance:

1. You must be at your work station, ready to work, by 8:00 a.m. each workday. If you are going to be late, you need to inform your manager before 8:00 a.m. You will also be expected to give your manager the time you expect to arrive. The next time you are late for work and fail to call in, you will be terminated.

2. You are expected to produce a signed doctor's note for your absence on September 24 within three working days of this notice. This note must be delivered to your manager no later than 5 p.m., October 8, 19XX. Failure to do so will result in termination.

Failure to meet any of these standards will result in immediate termination.

_____   _____
Employee   Date

_____   _____
Manager   Date

SAMPLE RELEASE AND WAIVER
(As It Relates to Termination)

DISCLAIMER: This is a sample release and waiver and does not pertain to all situations and conditions. All releases and waivers should be reviewed by legal counsel prior to implementation.

This release and waiver is made on the (day of month) of (name of month) by (name of employee) and (name of company).

1.   In consideration for the benefits granted to the undersigned by (name of company) as described in this agreement, the undersigned voluntarily releases the company from any and all debts, actions, demands, suits, claims and liability of every name and nature, both at law and inquity. The undersigned promises that he/she will not individually, or as a member of a class, hereafter, file any complaints, charges or claims against (name of the company), with any administrative, state, federal or governmental entity, agency or board, or any court action based on any action by (name of the company) which occurred prior to the date the undersigned signs this release and waiver.

2.   The undersigned represents to (name of the company) that he/she has been given the right to consult with legal counsel.

3.   This release and waiver does not extend to claims which the creditor does know or suspect to exist in his favor at the time of executing this release.

4.   The undersigned acknowledges and represents that in executing this release and waiver, he/she does not rely, and has not relied upon, any representation or statement not expressly set forth herein made by (name of company), its agents, employees or representatives with regard to the subject matter of this release and waiver.

5.   The conditions of this Release and Waiver are:

(Terms of agreement including any severance or any other compensation which will be due the undersigned. All terms and conditions should be specifically spelled out in detail.) In witness whereof, the undersigned has freely and knowingly executed this release and waiver on and as of the day and date set out above.

COMPANY NAME
Name: _____

Date: _____

UNDERSIGNED
Name: _____

Date: _____

ADDITIONAL RESOURCES

To explore further the issues related to difficult employees, the authors recommend:

Brounstein, Marty. *Handling the Difficult Employee: Solving Performance Problems.* Menlo Park, CA: Crisp Publications, Inc., 1993.

Robertson, Cliff. *Hire Right, Fire Right: A Manager's Guide to Employment Practices that Avoid Lawsuits.* New York, NY: McGraw-Hill, Inc., 1992.

Wylie, Peter, and Mardy Grothe. *Problem Employees: How to Improve Their Performance, A Step-by-Step Approach.* Dover, NH: Upstart Publishing, Inc., 1991.

NOTES

NOTES

NOTES

NOTES

OVER 150 BOOKS AND 35 VIDEOS AVAILABLE IN THE 50-MINUTE SERIES

We hope you enjoyed this book. If so, we have good news for you. This title is part of the best-selling *50-MINUTE™ Series* of books. All *Series* books are similar in size and identical in price. Many are supported with training videos.

To order *50-MINUTE* Books and Videos or request a free catalog, contact your local distributor or Crisp Publications, Inc., 1200 Hamilton Court, Menlo Park, CA 94025. Our toll-free number is (800) 442-7477.

50-Minute Series Books and Videos Subject Areas . . .

Management
Training
Human Resources
Customer Service and Sales Training
Communications
Small Business and Financial Planning
Creativity
Personal Development
Wellness
Adult Literacy and Learning
Career, Retirement and Life Planning

Other titles available from Crisp Publications in these categories

Crisp Computer Series
The Crisp Small Business & Entrepreneurship Series
Quick Read Series
Management
Personal Development
Retirement Planning